THE POCKET BOOK OF HEALING TREE MEDITATIONS

(LET GO OF STRESS BY CONNECTING WITH TREES AND NATURE)

JANEY BOWYER

For Dad

Printed in the United Kingdom

First Printing, 2019

ISBN 978-1-5272-3945-6

www.thewordsprite.com

❀ Created with Vellum

1. JANEY, NATURE AND HEALING

*L*ike many, my childhood was challenging. Instinctively even now I can't help but sew a silver lining into the seam of a problem. My friends described me as a Phoenix and I would say that is a fair description. As a consequence the takeaway I got from my past challenges was to eventually learn that I didn't have to be anything other than Janey. I didn't need to try and fit in as I discovered after many years of trying. A tree, after all, doesn't pretend to be a bee, so why should I pretend to be what I am not just to follow the norm?

It didn't help that school felt tough due to my dyslexia, back in a time before anyone knew what dyslexia was. In turn, I spent half of my life feeling inadequate until my early twenties when a chance buying of a second-hand yoga book, marked the start of my path of self-enquiry. At the same time, I started to study creative writing after work. The writing gave me hope.

I'm generation X, and we are the forgotten generation. We are the bridge between the baby boomers and the millenniums. I grew up wearing flared corduroy trousers in the 1970s when televisions and landlines were the technology of the time. Then in my twenties, I got my first mobile phone. For sure generation X embodies a time before high tech and yet are equally adept in today's world of everchanging electronics.

My sensitivity and the joy I feel around nature has led others to say that I remind them of a fairy. If I see a snail walking into the road or a trapped butterfly, I will always rescue them. I let spiders live in my home and give them the respect they need. I love all wildlife.

My Nan used to tell me she was the Queen of the fairies and the child in me still believes her, even if she is long departed from this world. When I was a young girl, once in her garden, I climbed high up a tree. It was fun until I fell and came tumbling down to reality with a thud. Thankfully, I wasn't injured, just a bit bruised but truthfully back then any salvation from my childhood life would come from connecting with nature and dreaming of fairies.

I would run to the fields and lay in the grass. Back in the not so far past when kids could safely do such things. I've kept up the habit of retreating to nature whenever I feel out of balance.

I can be sensitive at times. I know my boundaries and too much time spent in front of a computer leaves me feeling unbalanced, thus off for a walk I go in such times. I walk in the rain too. As long as I have waterproofs on, I am good to go.

I do feel that people have lost their connection with nature spirits, trees, plant life and the art of sitting underneath the canopy of a woodland; just allowing nature to do what she does best and nurture.

Yes, but I live in a city, I hear some of you say. Well, me too half the time, and in fact, the strongest connections I have had have been with urban nature.

It feels like the energy of elementals are coming into our cities. Never has there been such a time when we needed them more. They also have an interest; they want us to keep the trees and forest safe. I see elementals as positive nature energy and one that can be accessed by sitting near trees.

As you read this book, if bits sounds a bit too far fetched for you that is cool. Try the meditations and feel how they feel to you regardless of my words. Practice is worth much more than just reading about stuff. Let's commence.

One more thing: I offer ideas in a more accessible manner in a world that seems to be getting faster; I feel it is important not to lose intimacy with life. I love technology, but I don't think it should take over our lives. The internet can't give us a connection with nature that many of us badly need for the harmony of our being. So please remember to go outside and do the exercises.

2. WHY TREE HEALING MEDITATIONS?

*B*esides the beauty of trees, and the way they clean the air for us, as well as house wildlife, they offer even more if only we would take the time to get to know them. Did you know that trees grow better happier and healthier if part of a supportive tree network? So just like humans, they live on interconnection. Humans are also happier around trees. Try being around trees regularly and you will see what I mean.

Before sitting next to a tree and while walking in any place of nature it is wise to pick up litter and help keep the environment clean. Unfortunately, people still drop litter; it's not like humans don't know what a detrimental consequence such an action has on the environment. It was heart-breaking one time when I was on holiday in the New Forest when I found a family's entire eaten picnic left in the woods. They must have liked being around nature to travel so far into the forest; I can't understand why they would dump their plastic food packaging there.

Have you ever ran to sit underneath a tree to escape the heat of the midday sun? Cooler air means less pollution, also as the tree photosynthesises and draws energy from the sun and wind, it, in turn, purifies the air we breathe. Trees are smart and filter nasty pollutions from our atmosphere. They provide oxygen. In London, I feel the fact I have access to walk in the woods nothing short of a blessing. There are many kinds of forest and parks in cities if one would only leave the overused sanctuary of the sofa and visit them.

Mother Trees (essential key trees) are the older trees in forests. These key trees with the help of the mycelium network send CO_2 to the weaker trees in need. Trees will support each other no matter what, showing unconditional love. The older trees want the younger trees to flourish, just as the fungi also want the trees to succeed.

Fungi(Mycelium threads) form an underground internet offering assistance to trees. It is a two-way partnership, for Fungi also need sugar to live and hence like to grow in the ground near the trees. As the trees photosynthesise sugars from the sun, the fungi work to absorb the excess sugar, and in return, mycelium gives the tree roots water and nutrients from the soil. For seedling trees growing in the vicinity of mother trees, this offers a way of accessing a network that can't help but aid them to flourish. If key trees are cut down the rest of the forest suffers.

The whole of the magical underground world functions with a sense of unity. In many ways, this underground world has reached enlightenment. Some also believe this network has a consciousness.

Mycelium literary recycle energy, and the whole system feels like they are guardians, the fairies of the plant kingdom. Humankind is obsessed with the world through their own eyes that the world of the plants is often overlooked. The forest feels all about love, connection, inclusion, and joy. If only we hadn't lost some of these qualities in humankind.

Did you know Mycelium has been on this planet for around 1,300 million years whereas plants have only been here for 700 million years? I cannot help being blown away by this fact.

How do trees photosynthesis? Briefly, the roots of a tree absorb water, this water is then transported up to the leaves. Leaves contain chlorophyll. What happens is a chemical reaction as the leaves are also taking in carbon dioxide and air via their pores. Amazing or what! The light, carbon dioxide and chlorophyll then make sugars. The tree then releases the air, and the sugar is formed to feed the tree and also shared with the underground network.

Through my time of connecting with trees, I am convinced trees have different personalities. Some trees are wise and old, while others are fresh and versatile. Many trees offer a greater understanding as well as a bridge to universal energy. To tap into this energy, we need to come from a place of allowing and being. Patience is essential but above all, one has got to be like a tree, and to do this is where my workshops can help. I can take you on a journey into the magical world of nature and trees as you have never seen them before. For those of you who are not able to get to one of my workshops, fear not, this book is designed to take you into the world of nature healing.

Meditating with trees allows their healing energy and wisdom to reach us and hence ables us to embody our higher self. I feel trees communicate via their energy and hold much wisdom and history in a way that we may never fully understand.

Being with nature saved me from losing my direction and purpose in life. The natural world is my go-to place to calm my being. Trees give me meaning in life as I feel they understand me the most. As you do this work, I hope they can offer you the same and more!

Some trees I have more of a connection with than others. It depends on the tree's essence. High vibrational trees give of love and energy interconnected with the work I wish to offer the planet. They feel like humble messengers, cleansers that want to release us of our karmic past. Just as trees cleanse the air we breathe they have the potential to purify our thoughts, fears, and desires.

3. THE MAGIC OF LAWNS

*B*efore we sit and get cosy under a tree, I thought we should connect with a form of nature that is super easy for most to access. Even if you live in a flat, a patch of grass is available somewhere, be it in a park, or a public garden. My friend grows an indoor lawn for her house cat, and one could easily grow the same thing for a human. The reason for me wishing you to find a bit of lawn in some capacity is that I want to share with you my grass grounding meditation which I feel is a life saver. After all, too much desk sitting, stress and electrical things can leave one feeling unbalanced.

Sitting in the grass is a way to get a hug from nature. A lawn is also a kingdom within itself for insects and other kinds of creatures. Since childhood, I have loved lawns. They feel like a carpet of nature's ultimate grounding mat, bringing one out of stress and into calm. That's got to be a good thing. If you suffer from hay fever, a grass meditation may be too much and instead try walking.

When I first started to go deeper with nature meditations, I would sit in various parks and also go to the countryside. I felt the grass energy was unique and varied from spot to spot. I would experiment.

What was the same for all of these areas was their profound ability to ground me from the feet. Each place with their unique flavour and delicious after taste depending on where I parked my bottom. As time went by I realised each landscape for me had its own character, its elemental energy. The most robust connection ever was in Tintangle woods, but that is another story. The patches of grass near there are super-powered!

Grass grounding meditation has helped me every time I have needed it so I decided to add it to this book. My instincts told me to build a simple meditation that everyone from a cat to a king could do to feel better about things. Let's feel rather than read. Time to head out to a lawn or patch of grass of some sort and commence the meditation.

4. SIMPLE GRASS GROUNDING MEDITATION

ip: In summer I take my shoes off so I can feel the ground beneath my toes. For me, each time I do this, the moment my bare feet touch the grass I start to feel less anxious, more present and more in the now. Try it!

Method: Find a patch of grass to sit on in some capacity. Being comfortable is important.

Slowly start to breathe in and out the nose. Take your time; no need to rush. Close the eyes too.

Flare the nostrils and suck the air softly in, expand and softly exhale. No need to force but instead work with your diaphragm, so it moves down as the belly pushes out as you inhale. Then as you exhale, the diaphragm moves up. Continue.

Get used to enjoying the breathing, a slower sense of pace, the present connection with having to do nothing other than breathe consciously.

In the process start to feel the energy of the grass. Feel its creation, how its bright green colour provides a mini forest for insects to live and grow. The rich antioxidant surface provides cooling and a deeper connection with the earth.

Picture yourself reaching the world beneath the ground, the magical world of the unknown. As you sit there breathing slowly you can touch the grass with your fingers; you may even lay on your back and feel the grounding feeling along the length of your spine.

Feel green energy coming from the grass, grounding energy full of love. It coats your aura, it draws you down beneath, underneath it all to the centre of the earth. No matter what is going on in your life, this energy helps you to keep the peace. No matter how many emails you think you have to send, no matter where you feel you need to go, innocently allow the earth to nourish your being, to suck away your stress and to coat you with love. Feel the heartbeat of mother earth through your feet.

Ask the nature spirits of the grass to watch over you. Allow yourself to stay in their protection, breathing deeply and allowing life to unfold.

Touch the earth again and thank the grass for the help you have received today and for all future support.

Slowly start to come back and in your own time, open your eyes. You may wish to sit there for a while longer before returning to your day.

Do this meditation for five to thirty minutes, increasing the time with practice.

5. WOODLAND MEDITATION WALK

*L*ast week I went for a woodland walk in the woods that I hadn't visited before. When it is the first time I have connected with any tree or forest, I do so gradually. My eyes on this day were so wide open taking in the scenery that it felt impossible for me to be anywhere other than in the present moment. I was like a child witnessing a magical world for the very first time.

Nature is a massive healer. For me just being in nature has the power to make life feel better. Through stepping out of the electrical world of an office or home into fresh-air, it feels as soothing as a cold drink on a hot day.

Outside, I have often marinated my best ideas. Nature helps my nervous system to relax, and life feels less forced. Through letting go, my best ideas have appeared.

If you too have troubles, stresses and strains that you wish to let go off, try this walking meditation. A good meditation to fit into your weekly routine. The small time you give this will give you big returns. If it is the weekend perhaps, don't stay in bed and hide from the world, instead, wake up. The sun is shining, or even if it is not, nothing refreshes the soul like a walk in nature.

Things you will need: Comfortable shoes, waterproof clothing, water and make sure your phone is charged.

Method: Find somewhere you feel safe: a park is a good place. Walking in the woods can be fun, but if you are alone, you don't want to be looking over your shoulder every moment instead walk in a more public place where you feel relaxed.

Breathe deeply with every moment, making sure that you don't forget to exhale as well.

Take in the sights and smells of the park. The temperature and even how the ground feels under your feet as you walk. Try and use all your senses.

If you are lucky enough to have a park nearby you, you can even do this on your lunch break. You will go back to work feeling like a new you.

Remember you are the joy. Happiness is just one walk away.

Do this meditation for five to thirty minutes, increasing the time with practice.

6. FLOWER POWER MEDITATION

*L*et's talk about flowers now. Flowers are like kisses from mother nature, and I wanted to include a meditation that involved flowers as most people access them in some capacity. A flower can reach anyone. I remember when I was once bed bound for two weeks. I was told to stay in bed and lie down and do nothing. I stuck it out but felt miserable due to my lack of movement. My partner bought me a bunch of flowers, and they lifted my mood. I would stare at them, and they made me feel happier.

Not surprising as flowers are things of intense beauty and bring joy to the world. They remove carbon dioxide, help nature and insects to flourish and have a calming effect on our being.

Flower gazing meditation is a favourite of mine. If the weather is warm, you can do this in the garden. Choose a fresh flower/flowers with a nice long stem and petals that vibrate with colour and ideally are scented. The idea here is to use all the senses. The stronger the connection to the present moment, the less chance there is of overthinking and hence this offers a significant feeling of peace.

Method: Sit in a comfortable, cross-legged position or on a chair. Clear the energetic space around you with either incense or by asking whatever you believe in to watch over you. If you are not sure, you can always ask for the highest vibrational light to be your guardian as you do this meditation.

Next, hold the flower in your hands and get close to it. Smell it, with total awareness. Touch its petals, see how it smells and feels to touch and the beauty of what it looks like.

Be mesmerised by the flower and through it, feel your divine power.

Nothing else is needed now, simply be with the flower and allow whatever that is to unfold.

To end, thank the flower.

Do this meditation for five to thirty minutes, increasing the time with practice. An excellent way of connecting with nature without having to leave the house.

7. MY SHORT LIFE AS A FLOWER

(Inspired by Nature)

One life I was a little flower
stuck between two rocks
on a cliff facing out to sea

the sun warmed me
rain quenched my thirst
and the wind spread my pollen
so that other flowers could also 'be'

the simplicity of my existence
was without the complication of worry
for each moment I lived entirely 'in the now'

Insects collected my pollen
yet they were never greedy
and only ever took small feeds

each morning as the sun touched
my petals I felt that I could 'open up'
as the sound of the sea crashed beneath

at night the stars kept me company
the moon's energy acted as a lullaby
rocking me to sleep

one day my petals began to shred
and before I knew it, I was dead
for the rocks I was between fell

as my soul began to depart
I felt warmth for having lived
such a joyfully simple life

suddenly the wind carried me away
so high that I could no longer stay
what came next I do not recall

until one day I woke up to my mother's call
I was now a kid of mountain goat
running around a flowered scent field

8. FIVE LIFE CHANGING TREE HEALING MEDITATIONS

For ages, I would meditate with trees not knowing bar a few what kind they were. The rebel in me decided that trees didn't need a label. Deep down I knew I was missing out and I studied a bit and also did some tree and nature courses. This changed my understanding and helped me connect with trees even more.

I don't claim to be an expert on the names of every tree; however, I am glad I took the time to find out about tree species and their habits, especially of the trees that I visit regularly. I think knowing how they work helped me build a better connection.

When beginning this work, I recommend starting with one tree. The first one is like learning to drive; in the start things may feel confusing. Perhaps you like the idea of connecting with trees, but the reality feels forced and a little unnatural. Maybe the forest ground is muddy, and the wind offers the harsh reality that the task is hard. I promise you it won't be as difficult if you see it as an adventure. Enjoy the process and no need to rush.

Some of the pictures below were taken at the end of winter which is the hardest time to identify trees (for me), I am pleased I chose to do this at this time as it shows with a bit of patience, even in winter new connections can be made.

Many people ask me about how long to meditate with trees. My answer is simple: if you have half an hour, that is perfect. Even five minutes can make a difference. Be honest with yourself about your needs.

TREE 1

Healing name: The Elephant.

Appearance: Vast, grounding, bark the colour of elephants. Leaves were green but less than normal at the time of writing this as it was the end of winter.

Kind: Holm Oak.

Energy: Wisdom, protection, Abundance, Support.

Notes taken: There was a storm blowing early on that Sunday morning, and I was surprised to see a couple with a dog out walking. Lots of broken bits of trees were strung across the ground. The wind bit so coldly that I would have been forgiven If I had suddenly decided to turn back. This big tree stood out. It was extensive and old. While other trees flapped around in the gale, there was something about this one that invited me to stand near it.

The words that came to me were: there will be times of storms, times of peace, yet if I could connect with my inner light, my internal Oak tree, I could stand tall no matter what.

Meditation: Stand with your back to the broad trunk of this tree. Remember you are also infinite. Connect with the grounding energy of the elephant tree. Feel how strong and grounding the elephant tree spirit is, wise like Ganesha himself. Embrace how you can be an abundant being in harmony with all. Find the right balance of strength, courage and also allowing. Master your breath, master life. Therefore breathe consciously always. See how you are balanced in your being enough to respect that rest is as important as work. Find ways to relax outside TV. Remember the elephant is wise as he has big ears to listen. What sounds do you feel the tree wishes to share with you?

Sit and listen to the oak's majestic wisdom for as long as you need.

TREE 2

Appearance: A super head of green leaves and some red berries. A perfectly shaped tree. It reminded me of the character known as the Ghost of Christmas present from the Christmas Carol novel. A firm reminder of the abundance of life if only we would take the time to notice natures riches. A jolly tree!

Kind: Holly Tree.

Energy: Holy light, a crown to contain over thinking, surrender, sacrifice, rebirth, safe energy for the crown chakra. Jesus energy. Divine power.

Notes taken: I noticed that in the past sitting under this holly tree in my local park hasn't always been my first choice for fear of prickles. Its evergreen leaves offer a dense canopy that on this cloudy spring afternoon felt perfect. The weather was damp as I did my meditation underneath the spiky leaves. It became my home for an hour. I felt the energy of the tree reaching me from the crown of the Holly and felt the words: you are safe to be you.

Meditation: How can we learn to surrender without compromising ourselves? When are we brave enough to give our fears over to a force higher than our being? Think of a time when things got so severe that you were at a point where you knew there was nothing else that you could do than let go and work through the process by taking one day at a time. Make notes if need be.

Next, settle into your being and think of a time that brought you much peace and joy. Again feel free to make notes.

Continue by sitting quietly still beneath the crown of a glorious holly tree which has beauty in its green leaves, rich ideas in its fruit but a calmness of nature. You are safe to let the light in and guide you.

Sweet being, be still so that the crown of the tree can take away your worries. Know that if we work on our spiritual crown, our connection to source, our contact with the light, well the rest of life can start to unfold with much ease. It may not always go our way, but via surrender, we can reach the understanding that ultimately peace begins within.

Holly is a fantastic tree to help release spiky memories.

TREE 3

Healing name: Umbrella To The Stars.

Appearance: Tall, soft green needles with white surround. The bark is smooth.

Kind: Douglas Fir.

Energy: Truthfulness, being straight with yourself and to others about your needs. A clear direction in life. A pillar of strength, innate wisdom, resilient and hope. Keeping on track.

Notes taken: I love the way this tree grows up perfect in form. It looks well all year around. A precise tree that in many ways doesn't need too much description. Simplicity is the key. A tree of stability — for careers and reaching dreams through hard work. The words felt were: less is more.

Meditation: Sit beneath this tall spiritual master of a tree. A tree that knows whatever life throws its way that it still grows strong in one direction, up, up, up! The direction found in having a firm goal in life.

Stand tall in your truth and connect with the truthfulness of this pole long being. Feel how this tree adapts and still stands tall regardless of any surprises in life.

Your goals, pick a few, picture yourself working on them daily as you sit beneath this tree. Write them down if need be.

Next picture yourself growing up energetically as this tree does, growing high. Remember you are limitless and as long as you keep your feet planted on the ground.

Sit beneath this tree when every you need a little help with your career in life.

TREE 4

Healing name: Weeping Princess.

Appearance: Long flowing branches, textured bark, beautiful leaves.

Kind: Weeping Willow.

Energy: The link between water and land, the base chakra and sacral chakra, going with the flow, allowing emotions. The marriage of groundedness and flow.

Notes taken: I have often sat beneath this tree. It reminds me of childhood dreams. I adore the flow of the branches and how the willow dips them into the water and swims with the ducks. A queenlike tree. The roots of this tree are adaptable, and I have often sat on the ground feeling their presence. My secret hideaway. The words I felt were: flow is the key to joy.

Meditation: What is it that you need to release in your life? What emotions make you react rather than act? What tears have you sucked up into your heart when they need to be allowed to flow free?

Endings offer beginnings and beginnings endings. The cycle of life will pause for no one.

The weeping willow is most spectacular under the silver glow of the dreamy moonlit night. What dreams are you not following? Rest and allow Willow to bring you back into the flow. Even emotions can feel calm. The secret is not to deny them but instead become the observer by tapping into the water element of this tree.

Hush now, no need to be anything other than be at peace, peace with yourself and the world.

An excellent meditation for letting go of emotions.

Tree 5

Healing name: The Counsel of Birch.

Appearance: Old Birches with shredding skin but these trees have a beauty that is beyond skin deep. Multicoloured including salmon pink, white, grey and brown bark.

Kind: Birch trees (Growing in a circle).

Energy: A wise counsel. A strength through being soft enough to notice the things others often miss. Like stage deers resting to eat. Unity in numbers.

Notes taken:. I found comfort from sitting on the ground and feeling the mycelium going between each tree. The support they give each other and to others made this a special place. It felt like a time to listen rather than make requests. A time to sit with the high council of trees. The words that came were: wisdom in numbers.

Meditation: Sit around a group of trees and share your worries and cares, let it all out but don't ask for a solution instead allow yourself to feel the next step in life. Sometimes we need to just listen. Remember as a collective we are stronger. A group of trees offers the best knowledge as they are more supportive in numbers. Better than internet advice. Renew, listen and learn. Find peace in knowing the forest has your back.

Stay on this meditation for longer than other meditations if possible. It may take a bit of time to listen to a group of trees.

Now pick five trees of our own and do the same process, sit with them, connect with them, and find out what species they are.

Notes to take:

Tree Number:

Healing name:

Appearance:

Kind:

Notes taken:

Meditation:

Take regular walks in nature. Don't tell yourself you don't have time, instead make time. Even urban parks are rich with healing energy. Remember nature wants to work with us instead of against us. The more we can connect with nature, the better it is for everyone. Also, exercise is good for us, it is a win-win situation. Diary the time into your schedule and purchase some waterproofs.

Respect nature and be a lovely guest on this planet by leaving no mess. Try to buy things with less packaging and only buy what you need.

Bring more plants into your home to help purify the air and house.

Work with nature charities and find how you can give

back to nature for all that it does for you.

Find some local trees that you connect with and do regular meditations with.

Remember to study around five trees and learn their different personalities and which ones work with your energy.

Build up your meditation muscle by regularly practising and keep a diary of your findings. With time you will know which tree you want to connect with for a specific thing.

There is nothing like a lawn or grass to ground you when feeling frazzled. When I had a stressful office job, the park near my work is where I went to centre myself each lunch break. So if you are having a bad day then find a park.

Remember the healing power of flowers. The joy they bring.

Love nature, love yourself and love others.

Connect with me at THEWORDSPRITE.COM and look out for one of my tree healing workshops